Oxford Read and Di

Richard Northcott

Contents		

OXFORD
UNIVERSITY PRESS

OXFORD
UNIVERSITY PRESS

Great Clarendon Street, Oxford, OX2 6DP, United Kingdom

Oxford University Press is a department of the University of Oxford. It furthers the University's objective of excellence in research, scholarship, and education by publishing worldwide. Oxford is a registered trade mark of Oxford University Press in the UK and in certain other countries

© Oxford University Press 2013

The moral rights of the author have been asserted

First published in 2013

2017 2016 2015 2014 2013

10 9 8 7 6 5 4 3 2 1

ISBN: 978 0 19 464634 5

An Audio CD Pack containing this book and a CD is also available, ISBN 978 0 19 464644 4

The CD has a choice of American and British English recordings of the complete text.

An accompanying Activity Book is also available, ISBN 978 0 19 464655 0

Printed in China

This book is printed on paper from certified and well-managed sources.

ACKNOWLEDGEMENTS

Illustrations by: Kelly Kennedy pp.7; Alan Rowe pp.20, 21, 22, 23, 25, 26, 27, 30, 31.

The Publishers would also like to thank the following for their kind permission to reproduce photographs and other copyright material: Alamy pp.3 (stone sculpture/F1online digitale Bildagentur GmbH, sand sculpture/Phil Portus), 4 (Didi), 13 (lapis lazuli/PjrStudio), 15 (stone sculpture/F1online digitale Bildagentur GmbH, wood carver/LOOK Die Bildagentur der Fotografen GmbH), 18 (Ellen McKnight), 28 (stone sculpture/F1online digitale Bildagentur GmbH); The Bridgeman Art Library pp.3 (*Lion at Rest* (oil on canvas), Thayer, Abbott Handerson (1849–1921)/Delaware Art Museum, Wilmington, USA/Samuel and Mary R. Bancroft Memorial, *Lesson in the Garden*, 1900 (oil on canvas), Shirley-Fox, Ada (nee Holland) (fl.1887–1914)/Private Collection/© Gavin Graham Gallery, London, UK), 5 (*Still Life with Apples and Bananas*, c.1925 (w/c and graphite pencil on wove paper), Demuth, Charles (1883–1935)/Detroit Institute of Arts, USA/Bequest of Robert H. Tannahill, *Mount Fuji Under the Snow* (coloured engraving), Hokkei, Toyota (1780–1850)/Musee des Beaux-Arts, Angers, France/Giraudon), 6 (*Boy with a Dog*, c.1650, Murillo, Bartolome Esteban (1618–82)/Hermitage, St. Petersburg, Russia), 7 (*Lesson in the Garden*, 1900 (oil on canvas), Shirley-Fox, Ada (nee Holland) (fl.1887–1914)/Private Collection/© Gavin Graham Gallery, London, UK), 8 (*Lion at Rest* (oil on canvas), Thayer, Abbott Handerson (1849–1921)/Delaware Art Museum, Wilmington, USA/Samuel and Mary R. Bancroft Memorial), 9 (*Ducks by a Lake*, Thorburn, Archibald (1860–1935)/Private Collection/Photo © Christie's Images), 10 (*Classical landscape with boats on a lake below a castle* (black chalk, pen & brown ink on paper), Grimaldi, Giovanni Francesco (Il Bolognese) (1606–80)/Private Collection/Photo © Agnew's, London, UK), 11 (*Van Gogh's Bedroom at Arles*, 1889 (oil on canvas), Gogh, Vincent van (1853–90)/Musee d'Orsay, Paris, France/Giraudon), 13 (*View of Naples* (gouache on paper), German School, (19th century)/Private Collection/Joerg Hejkal), 16 (*Fabric collage of a football match in Peru* (textile), English School, (20th century)/National Football Museum, Preston, UK), 28 (*Ducks by a Lake*, Thorburn, Archibald (1860–1935)/Private Collection/Photo © Christie's Images, *Boy with a Dog*, c.1650, Murillo, Bartolome Esteban (1618–82)/Hermitage, St. Petersburg, Russia, *Van Gogh's Bedroom at Arles*, 1889 (oil on canvas), Gogh, Vincent van (1853–90)/Musee d'Orsay, Paris, France/Giraudon); Corbis p.14 (Mike Kemp/In Pictures); Getty Images pp.12 (purple/Phil Gatward, Jeremy Hopley/Dorling Kindersley), 19 and 28 (S Tauqueur/F1online); Naturepl.com p.9 ((bowerbird/Barrie Britton); Oxford University Press p.12 (palette/orange/green); © H A Schult pp.17, 28 (Arctic people sculpture).

Introduction

Artists make art. Art can be pictures or sculptures. Can you draw pictures? Maybe you're an artist, too.

What can you see in art?
Where can you see art?

Now read and discover more about art!

Artists

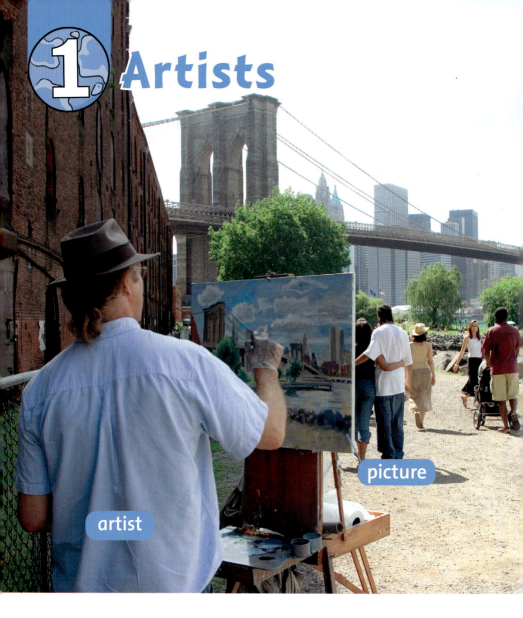

picture

artist

Artists look at our world. They look at people, animals, and things. We can look at art and see our world in a new way.

Artists like colors. Look at the red colors in this picture. What other colors can you see?

Artists like shapes. Look at this picture of a mountain. The mountain is in Japan. There aren't many colors in this picture, but there are nice shapes.

→ Go to page 20 for activities.

2 People

Many artists paint people. This picture is by an artist from Spain. There aren't many colors in this picture, but it's a nice picture. The boy is happy. He's with his dog.

This picture is by an artist from England. There are two girls and a boy. They are with a teacher, but they aren't at school. They are under a tree. The teacher is very young. Can you see the cat?

Discover!

Some artists look in a mirror and paint their face.

→ Go to page 21 for activities.

Animals

Can you stand by a lion? No, you can't! Lions are beautiful, but they can eat you. Can you stand by a picture of a lion? Yes, you can. Now you can see its eyes, its ears, and its fur.

Animals in art are great. You can stand by a picture of an animal and really look at the animal.

In this picture, there are six birds. They are by the ocean. You can see their reflections in the water.

Discover! This bird in Australia is an amazing artist. It makes a beautiful home!

→ Go to page 22 for activities.

4 Lines and Shapes

light lines   dark lines

Look at this picture of boats on a river. The artist draws dark lines for the boats, and light lines for the shadows on the water.

Artists draw lines with a pencil or a pen. They draw colored lines with a crayon.

Artists make shapes with lines and colors. There are lots of shapes in art. Look at this picture of a bedroom. Can you find these shapes?

→ Go to page 23 for activities.

paints

brush

palette

Some artists use brushes and paints. They put the paints on a palette.

Artists mix paints. They make new colors. Red and blue make purple. Blue and yellow make green. Red and yellow make orange.

Many artists like the color blue. Blue is the color of the sky. It's the color of the ocean, too. Look at all the blue colors in this picture.

Ultramarine is the name of a beautiful blue color. It comes from stones in Asia.

➔ Go to page 24 for activities.

6 Sculptures

Some artists use hammers and chisels. They make sculptures from stone.

These artists are in Cambodia. What color are the sculptures?

chisel

sculpture

hammer

You can see stone sculptures in parks. Stone is a good material for sculptures. It's good in hot weather and in cold, rainy weather.

Artists make sculptures from wood, too. This artist makes sculptures of goats. His sculptures are small, but they are great. Look at his chisels. There are lots of them.

→ Go to page 25 for activities.

7 Materials

Let's look at materials in art. Paper, stone, and wood are materials. Fabric is a material, too.

Some artists make pictures with fabric. This fabric picture is from Peru. It's a picture of a soccer game. There are 12 players. There are some fans, too. How many fans are there?

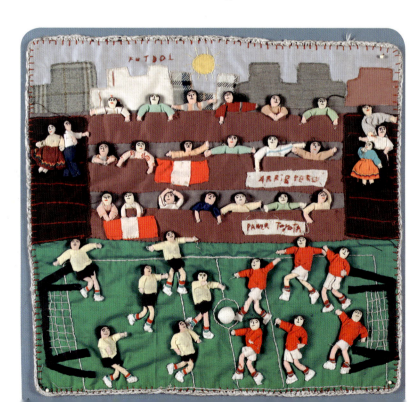

Some artists make sculptures with amazing materials. Look at these sculptures of people. What's the material in these sculptures? It's cans!

Discover! At the beach, artists make sculptures with sand. Here's a car!

→ Go to page 26 for activities.

8 Museums

Where can you see art? You can see art in museums. Many cities have a museum. One big museum is the Metropolitan Museum of Art in New York in the USA. Thousands of people go to this museum every week.

The Metropolitan Museum of Art

The Guggenheim Museum

Some museums are amazing. The Guggenheim Museum in Spain has amazing shapes. Can you find these shapes?

There are lots of books and websites about art and artists. Read more about art. Learn about great artists.

→ Go to page 27 for activities.

1 Artists

← Read pages 4–5.

1 Write the words.

> artist   colors   mountain
> animals   ~~world~~   shapes

1 _world_   2 _____   3 _____

4 _____   5 _____   6 _____

2 Circle the correct words.

1 **Artists** / Shapes look at our world.

2 We can look at **art** / **artist** and see our world in a new way.

3 Artists like **colors** / **new**.

4 Artists **like** / **are** shapes.

2 People

← Read pages 6–7.

1 Complete the sentences.

> boy   colors   happy   picture   ~~Spain~~

1 The picture of the boy is by an artist from
  ___Spain___ .

2 The boy is _____.

3 The _____ is with his dog.

4 There aren't many _____ in this picture.

5 The _____ of the boy is nice.

2 Complete the puzzle.

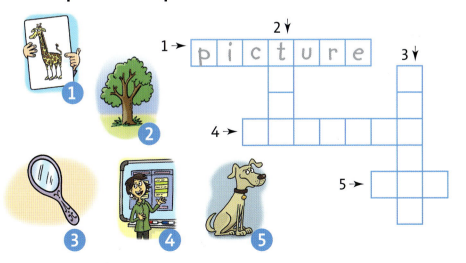

2↓

1→ | p | i | c | t | u | r | e |

3↓

4→

5→

3 Animals

← Read pages 8–9.

1 Write the words. Then match.

1 nilo

_____lion_____

2 yese

_____

3 ridb

_____

4 anoce

_____

2 Circle the correct words.

1 You **can** / **can't** stand by a lion.

2 You **can** / **can't** stand by a picture of a lion.

3 In the picture on page 9, there are **two** / **six** birds.

4 The **birds** / **lion** on page 9 are by the ocean.

4 Lines and Shapes

← Read pages 10–11.

1 **Complete the sentences.**

> artists   draw   pen   shapes

1 Some artists draw with a _____.

2 Artists _____ colored lines with a crayon.

3 Some _____ make shapes with lines and colors.

4 There are lots of _____ in art.

2 **Write the words.**

> bedroom   boat   pen   pencil

1 _____   3 _____

2 _____   4 _____

5 Colors

← Read pages 12–13.

1 Circle the correct words.

1   blue / purple / green

2   purple / yellow / green

3   red / blue / orange

4   green / purple / orange

5   orange / blue / red

2 Complete the sentences.

colors   sky   stones   yellow

1   Artists mix paints and make new _____.

2   Blue and _____ make green.

3   Blue is the color of the _____.

4   The color ultramarine comes from _____ in Asia.

6 Sculptures

← Read pages 14–15.

1 Write *true* or *false*.

1 There aren't any sculptures
   in Cambodia.   *false*

2 Stone is good for sculptures.   _____

3 You can't see stone sculptures
   in parks.   _____

4 Some artists make sculptures
   from wood.   _____

2 Write the words.

> goat   hammer   sculpture   wood

1 _____   3 _____

2 _____   4 _____

7 Materials

← Read pages 16–17.

1 Write the words. Then match.

1 a r c

_____

2 c r i b a f

_____

3 c h a b e

_____

4 a n c s

_____

2 Circle the correct words.

1 The picture of the soccer game is from **Japan** / **Peru**.

2 **Fabric** / **Sculpture** is a material.

3 Paper, stone, and wood are **materials** / **fabric**.

4 In the sculptures of the people, the material is **sand** / **cans**.

(8) Museums

← Read pages 18–19.

1 Complete the sentences.

Spain   museums   shapes   York

1 You can see art in _____.

2 The Metropolitan Museum of Art is in

New _____.

3 The Guggenheim Museum in _____,

has amazing _____.

2 Complete the puzzle.

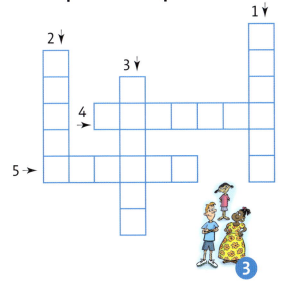

Art in this Book

1 Find this art in this book. Write the page number. Then write a word.

_____ page 17 _____

_____ people _____

_____

_____

_____

_____

_____

_____

_____

_____

_____

_____

2 Draw your favorite picture in this book.

3 Answer the questions about your favorite picture.

Are there any people?

_____

What other things are there?

_____

What colors are there?

_____

Are there any shapes?

_____

Picture Dictionary

animals

artist

beach

bedroom

boat

cans

city

fabric

face

fans

fur

goat

materials

mirror

mountain

museum

 ocean

 paint

 people

 picture

 player

 reflection

 river

 sand

 sculpture

 shadow

 shapes

 stone

 thousand

 website

 wood

 world

Oxford Read and Discover

Series Editor: Hazel Geatches • CLIL Adviser: John Clegg

Oxford Read and Discover graded readers are at six levels, for students from age 6 and older. They cover many topics within three subject areas, and support English across the curriculum, or Content and Language Integrated Learning (CLIL).

Available for each reader:
- Audio CD Pack (book & audio CD)
- Activity Book

Teaching notes & CLIL guidance: **www.oup.com/elt/teacher/readanddiscover**

Subject Area / Level	The World of Science & Technology	The Natural World	The World of Arts & Social Studies
1 — 300 headwords	• Eyes • Fruit • Trees • Wheels	• At the Beach • In the Sky • Wild Cats • Young Animals	• Art • Schools
2 — 450 headwords	• Electricity • Plastic • Sunny and Rainy • Your Body	• Camouflage • Earth • Farms • In the Mountains	• Cities • Jobs
3 — 600 headwords	• How We Make Products • Sound and Music • Super Structures • Your Five Senses	• Amazing Minibeasts • Animals in the Air • Life in Rainforests • Wonderful Water	• Festivals Around the World • Free Time Around the World
4 — 750 headwords	• All About Plants • How to Stay Healthy • Machines Then and Now • Why We Recycle	• All About Desert Life • All About Ocean Life • Animals at Night • Incredible Earth	• Animals in Art • Wonders of the Past
5 — 900 headwords	• Materials to Products • Medicine Then and Now • Transportation Then and Now • Wild Weather	• All About Islands • Animal Life Cycles • Exploring Our World • Great Migrations	• Homes Around the World • Our World in Art
6 — 1,050 headwords	• Cells and Microbes • Clothes Then and Now • Incredible Energy • Your Amazing Body	• All About Space • Caring for Our Planet • Earth Then and Now • Wonderful Ecosystems	• Food Around the World • Helping Around the World